Contents

Share in our story

Dancing Hares by Sophie Ryder in the Glasshouse Landscape at RHS Wisley

At a glance

240
acres of gardens for visitors to enjoy

Sandy
soil, which quickly dries out in summer, with occasional clay layers that can impede drainage

660
average annual rainfall in mm, over the past 30 years

24,050
plant taxa (scientifically classified groups of plants)

120
horticulturists caring for our gardens

Covering an area of 3,000m², the reimagined Oudolf Landscape contains 36,000 perennial plants of 162 different varieties

Brimming with horticultural inspiration and enjoyed by more than a million visitors each year, RHS Garden Wisley is one of the world's great gardens. From its iconic Mixed Borders to the edible wonders of the World Food Garden, and the botanical treasures in The Glasshouse to the cherished century-old landscape of the Rock Garden, there's something to delight young and old, beginner or expert gardeners. Innovation, experimentation and learning have always been at RHS Wisley's heart, and visitors can share in this exciting journey, whether from a workshop, a glimpse of the groundbreaking research being carried out at RHS Hilltop – The Home of Gardening Science, or taking home ideas to try.

Ethos of experimentation

From the outset, RHS Wisley has paired the art of planting with the science of horticulture, and combined learning with pleasure. George Fergusson Wilson, a businessman, scientist, inventor, keen gardener and former RHS treasurer, bought the original site in 1878 and established an experimental garden, forming ditches and mounds to create a range of growing conditions. His goal was to make 'difficult plants grow successfully' and the garden soon gained a reputation for its gentian, Japanese iris, lily, water plant and primula collections.

After Wilson's death in 1902, the RHS was keen to acquire the land – for some 30 years, it had wanted to move its garden from Chiswick, West London, to a larger site 'beyond the range of the London smoke'. Sir Thomas Hanbury, a wealthy Quaker and founder of the celebrated Italian Riviera garden of La Mortola, purchased the site (and adjoining Glebe Farm) and, in 1903, presented what became known as the Wisley

Did you know?

The first Award of Garden Merit (AGM) was given in 1922 to a *Hamamelis mollis* (Chinese witch hazel) at RHS Wisley.

estate in trust to the RHS for its perpetual use.

Here there was plenty of space to expand the RHS trials of flowers, fruit and vegetables, and 'endeavour to show to the public the best kinds of plants to grow'. To support the scientific and educational remit that Hanbury had specified in the transfer of deeds, a research laboratory was opened and the Wisley School of Horticulture founded, offering an intensive programme of study and practical experience. As early as 1820, the RHS had made plans for a 'National School for the propagation of horticultural knowledge' – but now purpose-built facilities allowed the School to expand and train a new generation of students. High standards, a wide range of opportunities for hands-on learning and close proximity to scientists conducting ground-breaking research meant that qualifications gained from RHS Wisley were well-respected.

Plant trials have also always been a fundamental element of RHS Wisley's work, with multiple selections of the same plant, or related groups, grown side-by-side for comparison. The results have helped generations of gardeners choose plants that perform exceptionally well in ordinary conditions. This important research continues in the Trials Garden and Edible Landscape.

Our Plant Heritage National Plant Collections

***Albizia julibrissin* cvs.**
best viewed late Jul–Aug

Calluna vulgaris
summer–autumn

Crocus Feb–Apr (spring) & Oct–Nov (autumn)

Daboecia
summer-autumn

***Daphne* (woodland spp. & cvs.)** all year

Epimedium Mar–May

Erica year-round

Eucryphia summer

***Ficus carica* cvs.**
summer–autumn

Hedera all year

Lagerstroemia Aug

Liriodendron Apr–Oct

***Magnolia grandiflora* cvs.** Jun–Sep

Metasequoia Apr–Oct

Parthenocissus
May–Oct

***Pelargonium* (spp. & hybrids, Stellar, Miniature Stellar, Dwarf Zonal, Zonartic)**
May–Aug

Ribes rubrum Jul–Aug

Sequoiadendron giganteum
all year

Shaping the future

RHS Wisley's educational and scientific capabilities were raised in 2021 with the completion of RHS Hilltop – the UK's only dedicated horticultural scientific centre. RHS botanists, taxonomists and plant health specialists are located here, collectively adding to a knowledge bank of how horticulture can, and will, affect our future. Already work has shown how garden plants can capture pollution, reduce flood damage and assist in cooling cities as our climate warms; current focuses include saving pollinators, identifying and managing pests and diseases, increasing plant biodiversity, and how gardening affects wellbeing.

As well as state-of-the-art research laboratories and botanical, insect and library collections, RHS Hilltop has facilities to share skills and knowledge. A permanent exhibition shows best practice to meet the challenges of gardening in a changing climate, and regular free talks, demonstrations and interactive sessions are also held. Through its Learning »

Studios for schools' programmes, educational gardens and an auditorium, the RHS aims to inspire and educate. From two-day beginners' workshops to a two-year course to gain a prestigious RHS Diploma in Horticultural Practice, RHS Wisley offers the chance for everyone to learn.

Astonishing biodiversity

With this ethos of exploration at its heart, and more than 120 years of planting, it's no surprise that RHS Wisley is the Society's most horticulturally diverse garden. A multitude of individual gardens have been created that, at the time of their construction, pushed the boundaries of horticultural excellence. The Rock Garden, one of the first areas to be developed in 1911–1912, celebrated Edwardian Britain's passion for planting alpines in a naturalistic style. The Glasshouse, with its incredible array of tropical and temperate plants, opened in 2007, capitalising on technological advancements that enabled closely monitored computer-controlled levels of heat and humidity. More recently, the Wellbeing, Wildlife and World Food Gardens are living laboratories that investigate and inspire the way we garden and display the results of our research.

Being a conduit for the creativity of many leading garden designers and landscape architects has also brought huge variety, from Sir Geoffrey Jellicoe's postmodern principles in the 1970s, Penelope Hobhouse's formal approach to cottage-garden planting in the 1990s and Tom Stuart-Smith's carefully balanced naturalism in the 2000s, to Piet Oudolf's 'New Perennial' style seen in his borders, reimagined in 2024.

The cumulative result of more than a century of such distinct and differing gardens is a plant collection that ranks among the largest in the world. RHS Wisley holds numerous National Plant Collections registered with conservation charity Plant Heritage (see panel, p7). It's also home to significant *Rhododendron* collections, with around 500 of the 1,000-plus types considered rare or endangered in cultivation. Similarly, *Camellia* is well represented with in excess of 300 types. A comprehensive collection of *Hamamelis* (witch hazel) brightens the shortest days of the year, and spring sees more than 200 magnolias burst into bloom. Then it's the turn of *Wisteria*, some towering into the tree canopies of Oakwood, followed later in summer by over 100 different cultivars of *Agapanthus* across the site.

In autumn RHS Wisley's fine trees come to the fore, more than 100 of which are the biggest (tallest or with the largest trunk circumference) of their kind in the British Isles, officially recorded as Champion Trees by *The Tree Register* of the British Isles.

Did you know?

Plants at RHS Wisley are grown peat-free, including specialist collections such as carnivorous plants that often grow in peat bogs.

Visitors wander beneath towering banana plants, bromeliads and climbers in The Glasshouse Tropical Zone

Evolving in a changing climate

Caring for such a wide range of plants brings challenges in the changing climate. We know UK summers will get hotter and drier, and winters milder and wetter – but RHS Wisley has always been a garden of experimentation, and we are adapting. Located in the south-east of England, this is a hot, dry site and plants have long been chosen accordingly. Some 50 years ago, *Tilia tomentosa* (silver lime) trees were selected for the Jubilee Arboretum avenue on account of their drought- and heat-tolerance; more recently, *Lagerstroemia* (crape myrtle) and

Known as the jewel in RHS Wisley's summer crown, the 128m-long Mixed Borders peak in July and August

Albizia julibrissin (Persian silk tree) collections have been built up as they suit the expected future climatic conditions. More than 6,500 of the 35,062 different plants housed across the five RHS Gardens are cited as critically endangered in cultivation, and we must safeguard our living collections and ensure they can thrive. One measure is to respect the old adage of 'right plant, right place'; if the environment becomes unsuitable, the plant is moved – the National Plant Collections of gooseberries and rhubarb, previously held at RHS Wisley, have been relocated to RHS Garden Bridgewater to benefit from the wetter conditions in the northwest of England.

Sustainability goals

Across the site, we are committed to caring for our planet, from making it easier for visitors and staff to reach us via sustainable transport, to supporting our wildlife.

Rainwater, a precious resource, is captured and stored, with Clear Lake dramatically increasing our water-storage capacity in 2023. Along with water extracted from the River Wey, this has enabled us to largely eliminate mains water from horticultural use. The vast majority of RHS Wisley is not irrigated: plants for the reimagined Oudolf Landscape were »

118,719

queries from home gardeners answered each year by the RHS Gardening Advice Service based at RHS Wisley

450

volunteers helping us by gardening, acting as tour guides and providing administrative support

110,000

packets of seeds, mostly gathered at RHS Wisley, annually distributed to RHS members and botanical institutions

95,006

dried plant specimens preserved in the RHS Herbarium at RHS Hilltop for botanical reference selected to require little or no watering once established. And where water is needed, we increasingly use soil-moisture monitoring to ensure it's used efficiently. Greywater will be made available for irrigation in the future.

Energy, too, is a primary consideration. Solar panels are used across the site, and air-source heat pumps in the Welcome Building provide heating and hot water. New buildings (and recently refurbished old ones) are highly insulated, and their design makes good use of daylight – with energy-efficient LEDs for supplementary lighting. Waste was minimised during their construction, too: 99 per cent of construction waste was recycled during the RHS Hilltop build. Unique solutions were sought for demanding requirements – the Herbarium walls are lined with Cornish clay and a hydrostatic liner which, together with a state-of-the-art air conditioning system, ensure the best environmental conditions for our priceless horticultural collections, delivered in an energy-efficient manner.

To support biodiversity, more than 400 trees have recently been planted, and bat and bird boxes, and bug hotels installed. Dead wood is left to feed staghorn and other beetles, and areas of bare soil support ground-nesting bees, including the native beewolf. The site is important for reptiles, including snakes and the rare sand lizard, and six bat species have been recorded here – a key indicator of a healthy ecosystem.

A garden destination

RHS Wisley's progressive, experimental approach has always drawn plenty of curious visitors. For the first 30 years, the garden was only open to RHS Fellows and their guests. Records show 5,250 visitors were welcomed in 1905 and, by the late 1920s, numbers had climbed to an impressive 48,000, despite what was then seen to be the site's remote, rural location. When the gates opened to the general public in 1934, people flocked to see the cutting-edge planting. By 1957, visitor numbers hit 170,000, surpassing 400,000 in 1978, 500,000 in 1985 and 600,000 in 1987.

Facilities have improved to accommodate the increasing footfall. In 1975 a gift shop and information centre replaced the souvenir kiosk, with a garden centre added in 1979. The £20million Welcome Building with eateries, shop and seating was officially opened in 2019.

RHS Wisley is a garden that looks to the future as well as the past, inspires and informs, and shares the best that horticulture has to offer. There's plenty more of RHS Wisley's story yet to tell: do visit again soon and follow our next chapter. o

Did you know?

Rainwater storage tanks under the car parks can hold enough water to fill three Olympic-sized swimming pools.

Euphorbia wallichii and *Dianthus carthusianorum* bring vibrant colour to the restful Wellbeing Garden at RHS Hilltop

Landmark moments

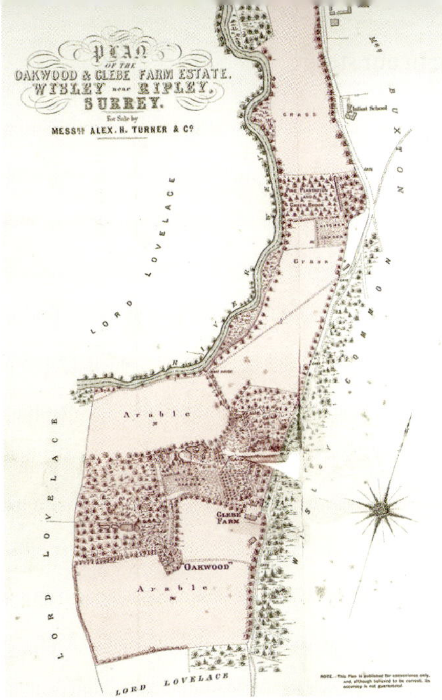

1878

George Fergusson Wilson buys an area of wooded farmland and rough pasture, and creates an experimental informal garden. Visitors include naturalist Alfred Russel Wallace, garden designer Gertrude Jekyll, horticulturists Ellen Willmott and EA Bowles, and suffragette Constance Lytton.

1903

Sir Thomas Hanbury gifts the Wisley estate to the RHS. The move from the RHS garden at Chiswick is completed in time to mark the RHS centenary and, in 1904, and the garden opens to RHS Fellows and their guests. Work soon starts on building glasshouses, where the Jellicoe Canal now stands.

1911

Specialist rock-garden firm James Pulham & Son complete the building of the Rock Garden to a plan by landscape architect Edward White. The engineering project requires the installation of a light railway from the nearest main road (now the A3) to transport 550 tons of Sussex sandstone.

1916

The Laboratory opens, built in Arts & Crafts style with materials recycled from old manor houses and designed to look as if it pre-dates the garden. It houses laboratories for scientific research into ornamental horticulture and plant health, lecture rooms for students and offices for staff.

»

1934

RHS Wisley opens to the public on weekdays, 10am to 7.30pm, or sunset if earlier, with Sundays reserved for RHS Fellows and their guests. In 1935, the *Journal of the Royal Horticultural Society* lists entry costs of 2s 6d for adults and 1s for under-15s (free to Fellows and their guests).

1939

When the Second World War breaks out, most of RHS Wisley's plant trials are halted to make space for food production. Demonstrations are run to help amateur gardeners increase productivity on their home plots, and the iconic Dig for Victory poster of a boot on a spade is shot at RHS Wisley.

1977

Almost 1,000 deciduous and evergreen trees from 90 different genera are planted in the Jubilee Arboretum to mark Queen Elizabeth II's Silver Jubilee. HM The Queen and HRH Prince Philip plant two specimens of columnar beech *Fagus sylvatica* 'Dawyck Purple' AGM.

2005

After 10 years of planning, the last of the 11,000m^2 of curved glass sheets is hoisted into place in The Glasshouse. Built to celebrate the RHS bicentenary and set in a contemporary landscape designed by Tom Stuart-Smith, the 12m-high structure took two years to construct.

2017

Work begins to construct the Welcome Building, with a restaurant, café, shop and garden centre positioned around a 'village square'. The £22million energy-efficient building is opened in 2019 by Alan Titchmarsh, with 98 percent of construction waste having been recycled.

2019

The final specimen of the existing collection in the RHS Herbarium is digitally imaged, following eight years of work and the recording of more than 92,000 items by the digitisation team. In the process, many treasures have been rediscovered, including a potato collected by Charles Darwin.

2021

RHS Hilltop – The Home of Gardening Science opens, a £35million building surrounded by 4 acres of living laboratories in the Wellbeing, Wildlife and World Food Gardens. The UK's first horticultural scientific centre of excellence protects the future of plants, people and the planet.

2024

Renowned Dutch landscape designer and plantsperson Piet Oudolf redevelops the Oudolf Landscape, 20 years after he first created it. A total of 150 volunteers help the Wisley curatorial team plant 36,000 plants in 3,000m^2 of beds in Oudolf's signature new perennial style.

Summer highlights at RHS Wisley include the Bowes-Lyon Rose Garden containing 4,000 perfumed roses

Explore the gardens

See the **map** on p75 and for accessibility information, visit rhs.org.uk/wisleyaccessibility

Welcome Landscape

ON THE MAP: 1

Designed by landscape architect Christopher Bradley-Hole and completed in 2019, the Welcome Landscape leads to the Welcome Building entrance. A colonnade avenue of 140 pale pink-flowering *Prunus × yedoensis* cherry trees creates a breathtaking spectacle in spring, and again in autumn when the leaves turn a fiery orange-red. Dune-like hummocks of clipped yew, beech and *Cotinus coggygria* 'Young Lady' AGM bring a modern feel, while existing treasures such as a 90-year-old cloud-pruned *Camellia japonica* 'Hikarugenji' were incorporated into the new design.

More than 250 native trees including silver birch, aspen and Scots pine have been planted in and around the car parks and a ribbon of perennial *Sesleria caerulea*, *Molinia caerulea* subsp. *caerulea* 'Moorhexe' AGM and *Sanguisorba* 'Tanna' divides the car parks and garden. To the east, contemporary tiered meadows are studded with topiary.

The Welcome Building sweeps you into the heart of the garden, and here you'll find a restaurant, café, shop and garden centre.

Did you know?

The old Wilks Gates beside the Laboratory formed the garden entrance for over a century.

A majestic avenue of flowering cherries provides a breathtaking spectacle en route to the Welcome Building

The iconic Laboratory building used recycled materials to age its design

Laboratory

ON THE MAP: 2

The Grade II-listed Laboratory building at the heart of RHS Wisley's story opened in 1916. It housed learning facilities for student gardeners and research labs for RHS scientists, and its walls have witnessed over a century of horticultural exploration and experimentation, and some defining moments in gardening history. After the Science Team moved to RHS Hilltop in 2021, the Laboratory was refurbished and now invites visitors to step back in time and enjoy fascinating glimpses into RHS Wisley's past with interactive exhibits and exhibitions from RHS archives displayed in the Gallery.

The outside of the Laboratory is wrapped with intriguing plants, particularly its west-facing façade. Because of the sheltering walls and eaves, plants that might struggle elsewhere flourish here. A treasured *Campsis* × *tagliabuana* 'Madame Galen' AGM (trumpet vine) has graced the walls for more than 65 years.

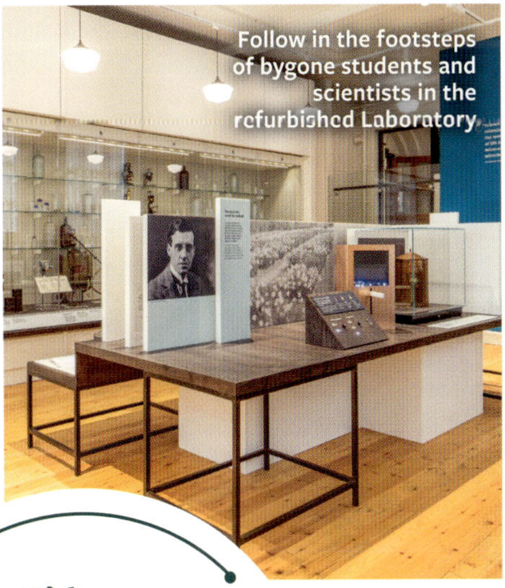

Follow in the footsteps of bygone students and scientists in the refurbished Laboratory

Did you know?

RHS Wisley resarch student James Kirkham Ramsbottom examined a disease affecting daffodil bulbs in 1916. He identified daffodil eelworm, immersed bulbs in hot water and saved the daffodil industry.

Framing the vista of the iconic Laboratory building, the Jellicoe Canal is home to a substantial collection of named waterlilies

Did you know?

The Waterlily Pavilion at the far end of the Canal used to be a potting shed, when a row of glasshouses occupied this area. It's now a stunning venue for wedding receptions and other memorable occasions.

Jellicoe Canal

ON THE MAP: 3

Built in the 1970s, the striking Jellicoe Canal, designed by landscape architect Sir Geoffrey Jellicoe, creates a formal garden area in front of the Laboratory. A collection of waterlily cultivars thrives in the Canal, and two raised pools house miniature *Nymphaea* cultivars ideal for smaller ponds. Both sides are planted with a cloud-pruned landscape of *Osmanthus* × *burkwoodii* AGM and *Lonicera ligustrina* var. *pileata*, inspired by a very old *Cotoneaster conspicuous* 'Decorus' AGM situated on the southernmost edge. Weeping *Cercis* and a majestic *Parrotia persica* (Persian ironwood) bring fiery foliage tints in autumn.

Conifer Lawn

ON THE MAP: 4

Home to some of the garden's oldest trees, the Conifer Lawn once held a collection of around 60 cypress trees, planted in the early 1900s. Most were felled in the 1987 Great Storm and severe storms in the 1990s, and the three largest conifers you see today are the only survivors. The two large golden *Chamaecyparis lawsoniana* 'Lutea' were considered a special find when they were planted here in 1989 and remain in fine health despite being struck by lightning.

The lawn is maintained as an open space to retain fabulous views to the Laboratory. This also allows good light levels for the swathes of vigorous large-flowered crocus that flower in spring – deep purple *Crocus* 'Flower Record', pure white *C.* 'Jeanne d'Arc' and purple-and-white-striped *C.* 'Pickwick'.

Planted with the help of visitors, thousands of crocuses are a magical sight in early spring

Just three of the original cypress trees remain, from the collection of 60 planted in the 1900s

Wisteria Walk

ON THE MAP: 5

Opened in 2018, the 75m-long and 3m-wide Wisteria Walk showcases two cultivars of *Wisteria floribunda* – dark purple 'Kokuryū' AGM and the delightful silvery-mauve 'Kimono' AGM. Now producing a tunnel of luxuriously long racemes in May, the wisteria took its time to bloom with late frosts repeatedly damaging the flower buds of the very early-flowering dark purple cultivar. In 2023, five years after it was planted, with the RHS Wisley Curatorial Team tending fire pits burning surplus wood to ward off frost on all-night vigils, it finally flowered. As our climate changes, this highly drought-resistant plant promises to produce an abundance of blooms.

Alongside the Walk, 16 other wisteria cultivars planted between the topiary present a full range of pinks, purples, blues and white.

Did you know?

Wisteria species have differing average lifespans. *Wisteria floribunda* is one of the longest-lived, and well-pruned plants can thrive for more than 100 years.

Planted between the topiary flanking the tunnel is a range of less-vigorous *Wisteria* cultivars in different colours

Long racemes of two-tone perfumed flowers give a wonderful sensory experience in late spring

The double Mixed Borders peak in high summer with vibrant dahlias, gladioli, heleniums and alstroemeria

Mixed Borders

ON THE MAP: 6

RHS Wisley's famous double Mixed Borders are among the finest in the country, a 128m-long horticultural extravaganza that evolves to bring bold colour and texture from late spring to autumn, reaching a peak in July and August. Extending along either side of the Broadwalk, on the slope up to Battleston Hill, they provide one of the garden's most iconic views.

Shrubs and trees provide a permanent foil around which the flowers come and go, and include *Paulownia tomentosa* (foxglove tree), *Catalpa bignonioides* 'Aurea' AGM (golden Indian bean tree), *Physocarpus opulifolius* 'Diabolo' (ninebark), *Sambucus nigra* (elder) and *Lagerstroemia indica* (crape myrtle).

The palette of perennials ranges from the cool colours of *Phlox*, *Nepeta*, *Agapanthus* and *Agastache* to the hot hues of *Helenium*, *Crocosmia* and *Kniphofia*. Don't miss the dramatic dinnerplate-sized summer flowers of *Hibiscus moscheutos* AGM hybrids, including Planet Griotte ('Tangri'), a favourite with our visitors!

These are supplemented by annuals as well as tender dahlias and salvias, which continue the show into autumn, joined by asters and hardy *Chrysanthemum* such as 'Hillside Apricot' which blooms into November.

Gardener's tip

Tall perennials are easily knocked over by rain and wind, so we build supports from locally-sourced birch stems and wire them early in the season. These are soon hidden by purple-flowered *Clematis* 'Jackmanii' AGM or *C.* 'Alba Luxurians' with white and green blooms.

Cottage Garden

ON THE MAP: 7

Beautifully chaotic, relaxed plantings soften the formal hard landscaping of this charming garden, designed by Penelope Hobhouse in the 1990s. She met the challenge of the sloping site by creating three level areas at different heights, linked with sloping paths to ensure easy access for all. A cascading water feature adds sound, while the surrounding catmints, lavender and *Syringa vulgaris* (lilac) cultivars bring scent. Plants from similar habitats and with the same needs are grouped together. An avenue of *Prunus itosakura* f. *ascendens* 'Rosea' AGM (rosebud cherry) flanks the garden, offering spring blossom and autumn colour, while eight arches are clothed in climbers. Through the growing season, the dominant colours change from misty blues, pinks and whites to glowing yellows, oranges and rusty reds.

Candyfloss pink blossom on the avenue of flowering rosebud cherries with daffodils and euphorbia in spring

Gardener's tip

Rosa 'Mulliganii', which bears clusters of banana-scented white flowers in early summer, grows over the arches. To extend interest, it's been paired with violet-blue *Clematis* Wisley ('Evip0001') AGM, which typically grows to 3m and blooms all through summer and into early autumn – when the rose's orange-red hips take over the show.

Compact *Rosa* Wild Thing ('Jactoose') AGM, pastel *Nepeta* 'Six Hills Giant' AGM and arches of *Rosa* 'Mulliganii' beside the cascading water feature

Exotic Garden

ON THE MAP: 8

A jungle of flamboyant leaves and vibrant flowers, the Exotic Garden showcases plants reminiscent of tropical landscapes that can flourish outdoors in a typical UK summer. Created in 2017 and designed by the RHS Wisley Curatorial Team, this area continues the garden's long history of experimentation. The backbone of palms and exotic conifers provide year-round theatre, while summer brings cannas, gingers, dahlias and *Tigridia* (tiger flowers); *Albizia julibrissin* offers a great example of climate-resilient planting.

The garden transitions from full sun, where thick groves of hardy bananas bask in the heat, to a shadier area with large ferns and foliage plants, showing what can be achieved in any garden. A maze of paths leads from the central fountain into the immersive planting.

Many plants stay in situ year-round. Some of the more tender specimens, such as *Musa basjoo* AGM (Japanese banana), are wrapped with straw to stop their stems from freezing, while cannas and gingers are given a thick mulch to help protect their fleshy rhizomes.

Did you know?

This garden contains a rare variegated *Trachycarpus* which is considered to be slow-growing, but this specimen is bucking the trend!

The flamboyant foliage of *Ensete ventricosum* 'Maurelii' AGM is complemented by spiky yellow dahlias, *Albizia julibrissin* with its pink, tassel-like flowers, purple-flowered hibiscus, and fiery red *Dicliptera sericea*

This inspiraitonal rose garden contains 150 different repeat-flowering roses mixed with perennials, bulbs, shrubs, grasses and clipped yew cylinders

Bowes-Lyon Rose Garden

ON THE MAP: 9

This innovative garden, begun in 2007, contains a range of resilient repeat-flowering roses, including climbers and ramblers, among bold drifts of herbaceous planting to encourage biodiversity. Spring brings *Camassia* and alliums; *Agapanthus* bloom in summer when the roses are at their spectacular best, followed by *Lagerstroemia* (crape myrtle) and *Crocosmia*; while in autumn, airy grasses are in full flower.

The garden incorporates the 1960s-style Pavilion, built to commemorate Sir David Bowes-Lyon (RHS President 1953–61).

Drink in the colour and scent of 4,000 roses at their spectacular best in summer

Gardener's tip

Trials with the Royal National Rose Society show that snapping off the dead flower just below the flower stalk is the most successful deadheading technique. Roses bear more blooms and produce new flushes sooner.

Spectacular displays of plants on trial can be seen in the Trials Garden

Trials Garden

ON THE MAP: 10

Trialling plants for garden performance has been integral to the work of the RHS since its earliest years, and trials have been carried out at RHS Wisley for more than a century. In 2021, the ornamental trials moved to the Trials Garden at the heart of the site, enabling visitors to see the spectacular displays of plants on trial, and discover new cultivars to grow. Multiple cultivars of the same plant are grown side-by-side for comparison over one, three or five years, regularly assessed by a panel of industry experts. Those that perform exceptionally well receive an Award of Garden Merit (AGM).

For the 2024 RHS Trial of *Muscari* in containers, 13 new AGMs and two existing AGMs were confirmed

RHS AWARD OF GARDEN MERIT

When plant shopping, look out for this logo on labels and in online descriptions. It indicates the plant has earned an Award of Garden Merit, allowing you to buy with confidence. The full list of current plant trials at RHS Wisley and other sites is at rhs.org.uk/trials

Don't miss!

The eastern perimeter of the garden hosts a hedging demonstration of 30 different planting choices, including evergreen, flowering and fruiting.

Providing a burst of spring colour, a ribbon of *Tiarella wherryi* AGM skirts around white-blooming *Rhododendron* 'Adonis' AGM and pink-flowered *R.* 'Caroline Allbrook', planted beneath *Staphylea colchica* 'Grandiflora'

Battleston Hill

ON THE MAP: 11

This beautiful woodland garden is best-known for its flamboyant burst of late-spring colour. The land was bought from the neighbouring Lovelace Estate in 1936 and, after the Second World War, planted with rhododendrons and azaleas; vast areas were replanted after the devastating storms of 1987 and 1990. There are now hundreds of rhododendrons and both evergreen and deciduous azaleas to admire, which all thrive on Wisley's acid soil. Collections of camellias and magnolias put on a joyful display from March to June, alongside the bright salmon-pink spring foliage of *Toona sinensis* 'Flamingo' (Chinese cedar).

The Broadwalk – the most formal part of the hill – is a plantsperson's delight all year round. Winding footpaths lead to discoveries of woodland plantings alongside spectacular groups of herbaceous plants such as agapanthus, lilies, *Hemerocallis* (dayliles) and hostas. Acers bring autumn colour, and winter reveals the beautiful bark of *Betula* (birch), *Castanea* (sweet chestnut), *Quercus* (oak) and *Stewartia*, while daphnes and *Hamamelis* (witch hazel) scent the air.

Step back to the Jurassic period as you wind your way through ancient plants in the tranquil Stumpery & Dell

Don't miss!

The Stumpery & Dell is full of ferns, tree ferns, ginkgos, hardy palms and Wollemi pines, and welcomes a wonderful array of wildlife.

Terraces have been created on the slopes of Battleston Hill, filled with sun-loving *Agave*, *Abutilon*, agapanthus, lavenders, *Eriobotrya*, *Grevillea* and *Callistemon*

Mediterranean Terraces

ON THE MAP: 12

With a south-facing aspect and sandy soil, the Mediterranean Terraces on the side of Battleston Hill provide the perfect conditions for plants from warmer climates such as Chile, New Zealand and South Africa, as well as some from the Med itself. As frost rolls downhill, this area also stays considerably warmer than many other parts of RHS Wisley in winter. The Terraces were created after the 1987 Great Storm felled most of the Scots pine that once stood here, exposing the slope to blistering sunshine. Several Australian eucalyptus enjoy the balmy conditions, the most notable being a towering multi-stem *Eucalyptus dalrympleana* AGM with ghostly white bark. Pencil cypress, winter-flowering mimosas and a fruiting *Eriobotrya japonica* AGM (loquat) thrive here, too. Many naturally have a high oil content in their leaves, and their scent is abundant in the air on a hot day.

The pungent scent of eucalyptus oil fills the air on balmy days from trees such as the multi-stemmed *E. dalrympleana* AGM

Gardener's tip

Frost always gathers at the lowest point of a slope, as cold air rolls to the bottom of an incline, just as water drains downhill. If you're experimenting with tender plants in your garden, place your plants outside of areas where frost pockets are likely to form.

Clear Lake

ON THE MAP: 13

An artificial lake with a capacity of 9 million litres, Clear Lake collects rainwater runoff from the roofs of RHS Hilltop. Holding the equivalent of 42,000 domestic butts, the water is used to irrigate the 10-acre Battleston Hill garden during dry spells. Gently sloping sides mean it's also a useful habitat for a wide range of creatures and plants, and a large fountain aids water quality through aeration. Along with the Glasshouse Lake and various underground water tanks, Clear Lake forms part of our aim to be water neutral by 2030.

Clear Lake was created on the site of the former trials fields in 2023

The huge Otterbine fountain helps mask traffic noise and its geyser-like spray captures oxygen molecules from the air to help aerate the water for wildlife

RHS Hilltop – The Home of Gardening Science

ON THE MAP: 14

The first dedicated horticultural scientific centre in the UK invites the world to see the RHS at work: witness research in progress, learn about our invaluable projects and enjoy world-class collections. The state-of-the-art building opened in 2021 and – with its enveloping Wellbeing, Wildlife and World Food Gardens – provides the facilities for us to research and share how we can all garden sustainably and help protect the future of plants, people and the planet together.

In three modern **laboratories** purpose-built for collaborative research, a 70-strong team of advisors, scientists and PhD students focus on finding solutions to the key environmental challenges gardeners face today. This research will be shared around the globe and influence policymakers in industry and government.

Two accessible **Learning Studios**, a **Learning Garden** and an **auditorium** welcome hundreds of schoolchildren every week, with hands-on guided workshops to support curriculum learning and inspire exploration of the natural world. This is where we train our future botanists and environmental scientists.

The spacious **atrium** hosts an exhibition to inform and inspire visitors, with behind-the-scenes tours and sessions with our gardeners, scientists and collection specialists.

RHS Hilltop is the base for the **Seed Team**, which collects, cleans and distributes seed to RHS members and botanical institutions. The **RHS Gardening Advice Service** team is also located here: visit rhs.org.uk/advice service to find out how to enlist their help.

The **Sky Terrace** gives a bird's-eye view over the surrounding landscape.

RHS Libraries collection

Preserving over 500 years of gardening history and science, the RHS Libraries collection contains more than 100,000 books, 30,000 botanical artworks, a large quantity of archives and 250,000 photographs. It is the most complete record of the UK's horticultural heritage. Everyone is welcome to browse, make research appointments and attend events, and RHS members can borrow resources from the lending library; parts of the collection can also be accessed online at rhs.org.uk/collections

Don't miss!

Join us for Hilltop Live, a regular series of free talks, demonstrations and interactive sessions. Visit rhs.org.uk/hilltop to see what's on.

Designed by Wilkinson Eyre architects, the £35million state-of-the-art RHS Hilltop building opened in 2021

The RHS Herbarium is environmentally controlled to ensure this unique record of plant diversity is preserved for the future

RHS Herbarium

With more than 95,000 specimens, the RHS Herbarium contains the world's largest dedicated collection of pressed and dried specimens of the UK's ornamental plants. A digitisation suite enables taxonomists, horticultural scientists and students to access and study the collection from anywhere in the world.

You can have a look for yourself by visiting rhs.org.uk/herbarium

The 1½-acre garden is filled with insect-friendly planting, sculptures and numerous ponds

Wildlife Garden

ON THE MAP: 15

Designed by Ann-Marie Powell and inspired by the structure of a bee's wing, this space is divided into many segments and packed with wildlife-friendly plants. The RHS Plants for Bugs Study showed that growing a diverse range of plants, with flowers in every month, is key to supporting local wildlife. Flowering hedges, swathes of plants from the RHS Plants for Pollinators list, 200 trees, 120,000 bulbs and a rough-cut meadow demonstrate how to achieve this, offering year-round food and habitat to a huge diversity of creatures. Log piles, bee nesting tubes, dead wood, a compost heap and a sculpture by Tom Hare add plenty of nooks for a range of creatures to call home. Two large ponds demonstrate aquatic and marginal planting, and a low bridge skimming the water's surface enables up-close viewing. You can enjoy watching this celebration of flora and fauna from the bird hide, and a smaller wildlife garden with a living roof and mini pond shows you how to easily replicate these ideas at home.

Designed to inspire visitors to reconnect with nature, the garden contains a diverse mix of flowering plants

Don't miss!

The Wildlife Garden is linked to the World Food Garden by a 2m-high hill, offering fabulous views over both gardens. Edibles are mixed into the planting on the connecting mound to serve as a reminder of the vital link between insect pollinators and our ability to grow fruit and vegetables.

Wellbeing Garden

ON THE MAP: 16

Did you know?

The design draws on the idea of RHS Hilltop being the metaphorical lungs breathing new life into RHS Wisley and the horticultural industry. The design of the garden is reminiscent of capillaries, allowing this to flow into the surrounding areas.

The link between gardening and wellbeing has long been known and the Wellbeing Garden is an experimental space that's helping us examine and better understand the positive effects of plants on people. Designed by Chelsea Gold medallist Matt Keightley, it opened in 2021.

The garden comprises a series of colour-themed 'rooms', planted to evoke a sense of calm in cool silvers and whites, then uplifting pastels, intensifying to more energised, high-summer hues of rusty-red *Helenium* and hot-orange *Kniphofia*. Scent has also been carefully considered with clipped pine and rosemary; spring brings the chocolate perfume of *Azara microphylla* AGM and, in autumn, *Cercidiphyllum japonicum* 'Rotfuchs' produces a candyfloss-like fragrance. A single *Gleditsia triacanthos* 'Rubylace' and *Liriodendron tulipifera* 'Aureomarginatum' AGM are planted on two elliptical white-stone terraces with clover lawns.

The design encourages flow around the garden with myriad paths offering an almost limitless number of routes. A scattering of *Styphnolobium japonicum* (Japanese pagoda trees) paired with drifts of *Pinus mugo* (dwarf mountain pines) subtly marks the route to RHS Hilltop.

Salvia nemorosa 'Amethyst' AGM and *Stipa gigantea* AGM feature in the calming vista of soft planting

RHS scientists are collating evidence of how visitors respond to the different parts of the Wellbeing Garden

Occupying the space of a former storage yard, the inspirational World Food Garden was completed in 2021

Kiwi fruits are among the abundance of tasty edible crops

World Food Garden

ON THE MAP: 17

A collaboration between RHS Chelsea Gold medal-winning garden designer Ann-Marie Powell and the Wisley Edibles Team, this 3,738m² (just shy of an acre) garden brings together fruit, vegetables, herbs and other edible plants. Beds of all shapes and sizes radiate from a central path running under arches adorned with a variety of climbing edibles, inspiring visitors to grow their own at home whether that's in a veggie bed, on a balcony or in an awkward corner.

The garden is split into three areas. **Good to Grow** displays a wide selection of fruit and perennial and annual vegetables, including many holding an Award of Garden Merit. The **World Maze** is home to lesser-known species such as Japanese wineberry (*Rubus phoenicolasius*) and American groundnut (*Apios americana*), and features tender plants such as the cucurbit achocha (*Cyclanthera pedata*), which may become more familiar as the climate warms. **Herb and Flower**, with café seating, reveals the wide variety of beautiful pollinator-friendly plants that can be used to flavour herbal teas, salads and all manner of dishes. The boundary of trained fruit demonstrates a range of different training methods.

Did you know?

The World Food Garden is managed without chemicals and operates a 'no dig' method of caring for the soil.

Fruit trees in the organically managed Orchard Landscape are interplanted with cornfield annuals

Edible Landscape

ON THE MAP: 18

An experimental garden of many parts, the 19-acre Edible Landscape showcases growing produce in harmony with nature. It focuses on fruit, and a mosaic of diverse habitats benefit wildlife and support healthier crops.

In the **Orchard Landscape**, many of the original apple trees planted in the late 1940s and early 1950s are being interplanted with a variety of fruits including pears, plums, apricots and peaches. These are arranged in groves rather than straight rows; meandering mown paths encourage exploration. Prunings are used to create dead hedges and log piles for habitat, ponds hold water in winter, grass is left long and studded with wildflowers, bare sand bowls benefit solitary bees, and a hive of wild honeybees buzzes with life. Different groundcover plants are being trialled, and mounds house resilient plants such as sweet rocket, oregano and fennel to feed both people and pollinators. Willow beds provide woodchip to mulch young trees and material for structures in the World Food Garden.

The **Allotments** provide an opportunity for community growers, youth groups and RHS Diploma students to develop and showcase their food growing skills.

Opened in 2024, the **Edible Trials Garden** trials a range of fruit and vegetable crops, and the best of these earn an Award of Garden Merit (see p29).

A range of traditional and unusual fruits, including our National Plant Collection of *Ribes rubrum* (redcurrant), grows in the

Gardener's tip

Creating a mosaic of different habitats and plant types in your garden helps to improve biodiversity both above and below ground, which in turn aids healthy crop production.

Fruit Garden, together with cut flowers and herbaceous perennials, interwoven with trees, shrubs and groundcover planting. This creates a rich polyculture, improving soil health and natural pest control, and offers a wealth of ideas that we hope you'll try in your own garden. There are also displays of trained fruit, and the glasshouse contains our National Plant Collection of *Ficus carica* (figs).

The **Figgery** wraps around the World Food Garden, where chicory mines minerals from deep in the soil profile and opens up the compacted ground. Gorse acts as a nurse plant, improving the soil so that, in future, the figs and other plants will grow tall and be fruitful.

Greener Skills Garden

ON THE MAP: 19

Equipping the next generation of horticulturists with sustainable skills, and inspiring visitors to garden in a more planet-friendly manner, the Greener Skills Garden demonstrates the latest findings backed by our Science Team. It opened in 2025 and its design was a collaboration between garden designer Dave Green, RHS New Shoots (an initiative supporting young peoples' careers in horticulture) and the Science Team. This outdoor learning space demonstrates how rainwater runoff can be channelled into a wildlife pond and rain garden, and how waste can be re-used with composting systems, dead hedging and homemade fertilisers, alongside other measures to boost biodiversity and help mitigate the effects of climate change.

Regular careers events are held in the Greener Skills Garden through the RHS New Shoots initiative that supports young people who want to work in horticulture

Jubilee Arboretum

ON THE MAP: 20

Often dubbed Wisley's best-kept secret, this quiet haven is a lovely spot for a picnic or stroll. It was created in 1977 to commemorate Queen Elizabeth II's Silver Jubilee and boasts almost 1,000 trees from more than 90 different genera. The entrance closest to Battleston Hill is marked by a magnificent avenue of *Tilia tomentosa* (silver limes). Two *Fagus sylvatica* 'Dawyck Purple' AGM beech trees, planted by the late Queen and Prince Philip to mark the opening of the Arboretum, stand proudly among other columnar trees.

The Arboretum helps you compare different groups of trees. In the first section, trees are arranged by common characteristics such as shape, colour and foliage and flower-type. In the second and third, species and cultivars of a particular genus are grouped together.

The Jubilee Arboretum offers the perfect place to choose the next tree for your own garden

Don't miss!

There's a wide range of insect life to see and hear in the species-rich meadow, managed for wildlife and biodiversity.

Back to Nature Garden

ON THE MAP: 21

This welcoming area with trees, relaxed planting and a wildflower meadow encourages children and families to have fun and engage with nature. There are two treehouses linked via an aerial walkway, swings, slides and trampolines, a hollow log for climbing on and crawling through, a stream with water pumps, dens in which to hide, a living willow pod, hidden burrow and giant sandpit.

Opened in 2019, the Back to Nature Garden was inspired by show gardens co-designed by the Duchess of Cambridge and Davies White Landscape Architects for RHS Chelsea Flower Show and RHS Hampton Court Palace Garden Festival. It supports the Princess of Wales' work to highlight how natural environments can help build foundations for positive physical and mental wellbeing, enabling children to develop skills for life through free play, building confidence, strength, creativity and resilience.

The family-friendly Back to Nature Garden seeks to inspire a love of the great outdoors

Oudolf Landscape

ON THE MAP: 22

Dutch garden designer and plantsperson Piet Oudolf originally created the borders here over 20 years ago, and returned in 2024 to reimagine their design. Now serpentine paths weave through bold drifts of flowering perennials and grasses, with glorious views to The Glasshouse. Oak benches encourage visitors to linger in this immersive landscape. One of the most significant examples of Oudolf's signature 'New Perennial' style in the UK, the planting covers an impressive 3,000m^2.

Did you know?

36,000 perennials were planted here, around 5,000 of them grown on-site. They were chosen for their climate resilience and wildlife benefit, as well as their ornamental appeal.

Enjoy the view from the fragrant Viewing Mount

Viewing Mount

The Viewing Mount offers fine views over the Oudolf Landscape and Edible Landscape. Alternating *Lavandula* x *intermedia* Olympia ('Downoly') and *L. angustifolia* 'Melissa Lilac' creates a striking spiral effect for visitors, and feeds pollinators.

Sinuous paths weave through the redesigned Oudolf Landscape which features block plantings of perennials in Piet Oudolf's signature style

Alpine Display Houses

ON THE MAP: 23

Treasures await in and around the two Alpine Display Houses, with species and cultivars from all over the world thriving in conditions that replicate the harsh climate of high mountain regions. In the wild, these plants survive by anchoring themselves in small spaces between rocks, using long roots to search for water and nutrients in the sparse soil, and growing low to the ground.

In the **Alpine Display House**, plants are grown in pots and sunk into raised sand-filled plunge beds, and rotated to show them at their peak. The **Alpine Cushion House** has permanent displays and was renovated in 2022–23, now enjoying automatic ventilation and shading. Sussex sandstone and tufa (a porous sedimentary rock) have been used to create a range of niches, gullies and cliffs that suit the specific needs of different alpine plants. Drystone walls, sinks, troughs and the Crevice Garden are planted with cultivars that can be grown in limited space outdoors.

Sitting at the summit of the Rock Garden, the two Alpine Display Houses contain species from all over the world

Autumn-flowering plants in the Alpine Display House

Herons Bonsai Walk

ON THE MAP: 24

These evergreen, deciduous and flowering bonsai trees range in age from 40–100 years. Make sure to revisit the Walk through the changing seasons – just like trees growing naturally, many have spring blossom and autumn colour, and in some cases produce fruits and cones. Maintained in partnership with world-renowned bonsai grower Peter Chan of Herons Bonsai, Surrey, these fine living sculptures are the result of many years of expert training, pruning and precision cultivation.

The miniature trees in Herons Bonsai Walk are raised on stands to allow closer inspection

Did you know?

While bonsai trees are often sold as houseplants, many of these plants are hardy trees which can grow and flourish outdoors in a typical UK climate.

Unusual and intriguing plants feature in this area that commemorates renowned plantsperson EA Bowles

Bowles' Corner

ON THE MAP: 25

This area commemorates plantsperson and former RHS President Edward Augustus Bowles (1865–1954), who loved unusual plants. He was fascinated by what he called 'demented' plants – those with an unusual appearance or habit, particularly variegated and contorted plants. Bowles' Corner is home to many such favourites, and some that he bred or were named in his honour. It also includes plants likely to have intrigued Bowles if he were alive today, such as *Robinia pseudoacacia* 'Lace Lady' with twisted stems and curly leaves, and *Sophora* 'Little Baby' with zigzag branches.

Look out for snowdrops in February, (Bowles coined the term 'Galanthophile') and the sweetly-scented blooms of strikingly variegated *Daphne odora* 'Mae-jima'. By March, crocuses – another of Bowles' passions – carpet the ground and the fragrant flowers of *Illicium simonsii* fill the air.

Did you know?

Weather Hill Cottage was built by George Fergusson Wilson in the late 1880s and is an early example of a prefabricated building.

Alpine Meadow

ON THE MAP: 26

The grassy slope next to the Rock Garden is the Alpine Meadow, created in the late 1920s and famous for its spring and autumn bulbs. After a show of snowdrops on the uppermost ridges, *Crocus tommasinianus* AGM (early crocus) and *C. vernus* create a carpet of blue in late winter and early spring. Thousands of *Narcissus bulbocodium* AGM (hoop petticoat daffodil) bloom in mid spring and conditions are also perfect for *Erythronium dens-canis* (dog's tooth violet), *Fritillaria meleagris* AGM (snake's head fritillary) and anemones. In late spring and early summer, *Dactylorhiza* orchids appear, followed by yellow rattle.

Once the bulbs finish flowering, the grass is left uncut to allow seeds to drop to the soil, then mown closely before *Crocus speciosus* AGM (autumn-flowering crocus) appears.

Thousands of hoop petticoat daffodils cascade down the grassy slopes of the Alpine Meadow in mid-spring

Rock Garden

ON THE MAP: 27

One of the first major projects undertaken at RHS Wisley was the Rock Garden, built between January and August 1911. This ambitious engineering project was constructed by James Pulham and Son, specialists in large-scale rock gardens, to designs by landscape architect Edward White. A wide range of alpines and plants that flourish in alpine conditions grow here, and you can enjoy a number of special collections including *Hepatica*, *Crocus*, *Cyclamen* and *Saxifraga*. The steep north-facing slope suits plants that prefer a cool, shady spot, though winter cold and damp mean sharp drainage and skilful management is vital; sun-loving plants enjoy the more exposed outcrops.

Numerous small paths wind down and around the rocky outcrops, and pools are linked by streams and cascades. The water eventually flows into the Long Ponds where, in late spring, the bridge is draped with *Wisteria*. *Iris pseudacorus* (yellow flag) and Asian candelabra primulas thrive in the moist soil nearby.

Many original features remain, including a grotto with flourishing ferns such as *Matteuccia struthiopteris* AGM (shuttlecock fern) and *Osmunda cinnamomea* AGM (cinnamon fern). The dramatic waterfall and its Japanese-style landscape was added in 2004, designed by Professor Masao Fukuhara.

On the edge of the Rock Garden, the Fern Glade celebrates the diversity of ferns and many other plants that thrive in shady conditions. It's a favourite spot in early spring, when swathes of snowdrops flower.

Did you know?

The original orientation of the quarried Sussex sandstone blocks was preserved when they were positioned in the Rock Garden, to ensure a natural appearance.

Small weeping trees and dwarf conifers provide year-round interest in the Rock Garden with pockets of colour from seasonal flowering plants

Glasshouse Landscape

ON THE MAP: 28

A sweeping contemporary landscape, originally laid out by Tom Stuart-Smith in 2007, wraps around The Glasshouse and links it to the wider garden. The tall beech tree (Wisley's largest) on the edge of Oakwood is carried into the garden design with clipped beech hedges and cylinders; *Bergenia* (elephant's ears) and hellebores echo Oakwood's damp woodland planting. This lush green scheme gradually becomes more arid to mirror the interior planting of The Glasshouse's temperate zone.

On the far western edge of the Landscape, the South African Meadow features hardy perennials native to South Africa. In areas such as the Drakensburg Mountains, the

Structural hedges in the Glasshouse Landscape are illuminated on a frosty morning as the sun rises over the lake

Clipped beech columns and a sea of bleached *Miscanthus* frame Sophie Ryder's *Dancing Hares* sculpture

combination of high summer rainfall and the threat of wildlife creates a tough environment for plants, resulting in a unique range of adapted flora. Key plants include *Berkheya purpurea* with its striking purple blooms, *Watsonia pillansii* bringing splashes of vibrant orange, and *Kniphofia caulescens*, one of the most distinctive red-hot pokers.

Don't miss!

The dramatic yellow umbels of *Ferula communis* (giant fennel) attract clouds of pollinators in late spring, and its structural seedheads last into winter.

The Glasshouse

ON THE MAP: 29

The cathedral-like Glasshouse, covering the area of 10 tennis courts and rising to 12m high, opened in 2007 to celebrate the bicentenary of the RHS and houses its world-class collection of tender plants. Here many difficult-to-grow, rare and endangered species thrive in the controlled conditions, and there are three climactic zones to explore: Moist Temperate, Dry Temperate and Tropical.

The shadier east side of The Glasshouse is home to the **Moist Temperate** zone and native plants of temperate forests from South America and Australasia. Humid conditions are vital to this cloud forest environment, and a waterfall adds to the subtropical experience.

In the **Dry Temperate** zone, a scree and rock-strewn landscape mimics semi-arid and desert environments. It contains a rich diversity of tough, slow-growing, often prickly and strangely beautiful plants, all adapted to conserve every drop of moisture. Drought-tolerant plants from Chile, Madagascar, the Canary Islands, South Africa and Australia all thrive here.

The lush planting in the steamy **Tropical** zone includes palm trees, bananas, aroids, bromeliads and fast-growing climbers. Tropical waterlilies and other aquatic and wetland plants bask in the warm jungle pool.

Orchid House

In 2023, the Orchid House was added to house RHS Wisley's collection of over 3,000 orchids. A naturalistic setting mimics how they naturally grow on the ground, in trees and on rocks. Alongside popular *Cymbidium* and *Dendrobium*, rare specimens such as *Cynorkis uncinata* 'Rose of Madagascar' and seasonal orchids are rotated into the display as they peak.

Gardener's tip

Many familiar houseplants grow here, though on a much bigger scale. The plants in the temperate zones illustrate what will grow well in a cool conservatory, while those in the tropical zone prefer warmer living-room conditions. Plants found in the understorey are suitable for shadier parts of the home.

Huge leaves, extravagant flowers and fast growth abounds in the hot and steamy Tropical zone, where plants need regular pruning to keep them to size

Oakwood

ON THE MAP: 30

Formerly known as the Wild Garden, Oakwood is the historic heart of RHS Wisley. Here, George Fergusson Wilson created the original garden, creating diverse conditions to grow difficult plants successfully in a naturalistic style. It is now home to some of the most diverse planting at RHS Wisley. The fertile soil, high water table and light shade accommodate a vast range of woodlanders including primulas, trilliums and hostas. Lower-growing trees and shrubs fill the middle vegetation layer and rhododendrons, camellias and magnolias provide glorious spring colour.

Colourful candelabra primulas, tall foxgloves and stately *Cardiocrinum giganteum* (giant Himalayan lily) follow in early summer with *Rosa* 'Paul's Himalayan Musk' AGM clambering into the canopy above. Oakwood then sparkles with new flowers as the large, well-scented blooms of *Camellia sasanqua* 'Alba' open in November and December while spidery *Hamamelis* (witch hazel) flowers perfume the air in late winter.

A vibrant stand of *Iris* 'Caesar's Brother' beside *Davidia involucrata* 'Crimson Spring' and *Indigofera himalayensis* 'Silk Road'

Don't miss!

A century-old wisteria planted in Wilson's time now reaches 20m high into the oak canopy, creating a must-see spectacle in May.

Rhododendron 'Goldsworth Crimson' and 'Myosotis' dazzle in Oakwood at springtime

Walled Gardens

ON THE MAP: 31

Wisley's walled garden is divided by a yew hedge into two areas, East and West, each with a distinct scheme. Located behind the Waterlily Pavilion at the far end of the Jellicoe Canal, the **Walled Garden East** features a parterre, begun in 2016, that trials alternatives to traditional *Buxus* (box) hedges. The evergreen and semi-evergreen dwarf shrubs all have small leaves for better clipping, and cultivars that don't perform well are replaced as the experiment continues.

The **Walled Garden West** profiles creative effects achieved with flamboyant foliage plants such as hostas, *Bergenia ciliata* 'Wilton', *Adiantum venustum* AGM, *Muehlenbeckia astonii*, *Euonymus fortunei* 'Kewensis' and *Aralia elata* 'Aureovariegata' AGM. Yew topiary cones add winter structure together with shrubby cultivars of *Ginkgo biloba* such as curious 'Saratoga' AGM with deeply-cut leaves. A large *Trachycarpus fortunei* AGM (Chusan palm) remains from the area's previous tropical-themed planting.

Conifers, leafy plants and grasses create interesting foliage effects in the Walled Garden West

Gardener's tip

To create a diverse tapestry of leaf colours and forms, layer from the ground up. Mix groundcover with perennials of different heights and small shrubs and trees, and cloak walls and palm-tree trunks with climbers.

An eye-catching display of the trial of alternative hedging plants in the Walled Garden East

Seven Acres & Winter Walk

ON THE MAP: 32

Bordered by the River Wey, Seven Acres is a waterside landscape studded with wonderful trees, including a *Tilia henryana* 'Arnold Select' planted to celebrate the Coronation of King Charles III in 2023.

A lake and a smaller 'Round Pond' are separated by a grass causeway with a small weir. Sculptures of two cranes by Gail Runyon Perry seem to dance on the surface of the lake, and on the bank is the Butterfly Lovers' Pavilion, originally built for the 2005 RHS Hampton Court Palace Flower Show. In autumn, the area is ablaze with fire-bright foliage including the fine palm-shaped leaves of *Liquidambar styraciflua* 'Wisley King' (sweet gum) which flush a rich purple-red. The needles of deciduous conifers *Taxodium distichum* and *Metasequoia glyptostroboides* change to a bronzed orange tone before they drop to carpet the ground below.

Fiery *Cornus* stems add splashes of scarlet among the winter silhouettes reflected in the Seven Acres lake

Gardener's tip

Young dogwood and willow stems have the best colour so hard-prune them at the end of March, then feed generously to help them recover, for a vibrant winter display.

The Winter Walk leads among plants chosen for winter colour, structure, shape and scent. The textural snakebark maple trunks such as *Acer davidii* Viper ('Mindavi') contrast with the glossy red bark of *Prunus serrula* (Tibetan cherry) and scarlet stems of *Cornus alba* Baton Rouge ('Minbat'). Fragrance from daphnes and *Hamamelis* (witch hazel) fills the air, and iris and hellebores enrich the scene.

Equinox Borders

ON THE MAP: 33

Designed to peak in spring and again in autumn, the Equinox Borders were opened in 2017. Taking centre stage in spring are *Allium jesdianum* 'Early Emperor' AGM and *A.* 'Mont Blanc', and fragrant double *Paeonia lactiflora* 'Laura Dessert'. Among the autumn stars are asters, *Kniphofia* (red-hot poker), hardy fuchsias and *Hesperantha* (crimson flag lily) alongside *Parthenocissus* (Boston ivy) scrambling up the pine tree trunks, and curious seedpods of *Euonymus hamiltonianus* 'Rising Sun' and 'Popcorn'.

There's plenty to enjoy in other seasons with *Cotinus coggygria* Golden Spirit ('Ancot') AGM bringing a kaleidoscope of colours from spring to autumn and coppiced *Liriodendron* (tulip trees) adding a punctuation of summer foliage.

Autumn colour in the Equinox Borders

Pinetum & Riverside Walk

ON THE MAP: 34

The Pinetum is home to RHS Wisley's oldest tree collection with some of the *Pinus nigra* (black pines) planted by the garden's original owner, George Fergusson Wilson. The magnificent redwoods were added around 1904 with *Sequoia sempervirens* AGM (coastal redwood) the tallest at 36m. Look out for the huge *Pinus* × *holfordiana* (hybrid white pine) cones usually visible in the upper parts of the tree, and the prickly elegant foliage of *Cunninghamia lanceolata* (Chinese fir), often mistaken for a monkey puzzle tree. Stand beneath the trees and admire their grandeur, then climb Battleston Hill to enjoy a bird's-eye view.

Bordering the River Wey, the Riverside Walk opens in summer and is a lovely spot to enjoy a picnic, with kingfishers, herons and swans as well as dragonflies and damselflies sharing this peaceful retreat. Trees such as *Alnus glutinosa* (common alder), weeping willows, *Betula nigra* (river birch) and *Taxodium* (cypress) trees have been planted on the woodland banks, where native bluebells are being re-established.

Did you know?

The huge pyramid of zebra-like striped foliage in the Pinetum is a variegated *Thuja plicata* 'Zebrina' AGM (western red cedar), which is the largest example in the British Isles.

Visit RHS Wisley's oldest tree collection in the Pinetum

The tranquil Riverside Walk is the perfect spot for a summer picnic

Upright conifers, spiky yuccas and cardoons make unusual planting companions

Heather Landscape

ON THE MAP: 35

RHS Wisley has long been a home for heather, since one-time director Frank Chittenden amassed a collection in the 1920s, and around 25,000 heathers, including 900 cultivars – 162 of which are considered endangered in cultivation – can be found in this National Plant Collection. Redesigned in ribbons of colour, *Calluna*, *Daboecia* and *Erica* are shown in an inspiring new light, planted with *Yucca rostrata* and globe artichokes which also thrive in the sandy soil and full sun. In spring and autumn, the abundance of heather flowers provide valuable nectar for the free-living honeybees in the Rocket Hives.

This garden is set within the wider Howard's Field landscape, named after a farmer who once held the grazing rights to this land.

Gardener's tip

Removed plant material has been used to create structures for wildlife, including solitary bees, to live in, and this is an easy way to create more habitat in your own garden.

Planted in painterly ribbons of colour, the Heather Landscape demonstrates inspiring ways to grow *Erica*, *Calluna* and *Daboecia*

Grass Garden

ON THE MAP: 36

Inspired by the rolling sand dunes of coastal landscapes, sweeping borders showcase a huge range of drought-tolerant ornamental grasses from ground-hugging *Luzula sylvatica* 'Aurea' to 3m-high *Miscanthus* × *giganteus*. The flowers of *Pennisetum alopecuroides* 'Red Head' AGM (Chinese fountain grass) are a firm favourite with visitors, while the scale of the landscape allows grand clumps of *Cortaderia* (pampas grass) to reach their potential, to spectacular effect. Grasses for shade, including cultivars from the *Carex* EverColor Series, thrive under the high canopies of two mature oaks.

This garden reaches a peak in late summer and autumn, and there are also architectural companion plants to enjoy.

Backlit by the low autumn sun, the silky seedheads of *Miscanthus*, *Stipa* and *Cortaderia* sparkle in the Grass Garden

The sunbaked, south-facing Resilience Garden hosts plants that thrive in this challenging environment

Resilience Garden

ON THE MAP: 37

The new Resilience Garden explores the art and science of gardening in our increasingly hot and dry climatic conditions. Sunbaked and south-facing on Wisley's well-draining sandy soil, an area of recycled shingle aggregate hosts plants that thrive in this challenging environment with perennials such as *Echinops* and *Stachys*, and small shrubs including *Pseudodictamnus mediterraneus* (false dittany) and shrubby salvias. Part of RHS Wisley's National Plant Collection of *Lavandula* grows here, which contains more than 50 cultivars of *Lavandula* × *chaytoriae* and *L.* × *intermedia*.

The plantings are managed more freely than in some of the more formal areas with self-seeding plants, such as *Eschscholzia californica* 'Ivory Castle' and *Papaver somniferum* 'Lauren's Grape', allowed to find their own niches and naturalise. This species-rich garden not only showcases the resilience of plants growing in nutrient-poor conditions, but also provides a feast for pollinating insects.

The Stone Pine Café is named after the Champion Tree *Pinus pinea* AGM that stands over it, with surrounding Mediterranean planting including pencil cypress, olive trees and *Santolina*, and views over this arresting arid landscape.

Gravel gardening

This garden was planted with young plants in pots no bigger than 9cm so they adapt to the environmental stresses, often forming deep root systems. The layer of gravel acts as a mulch to retain soil moisture, so they receive no extra water once established. The plants don't grow as tall as their irrigated counterparts, reducing the need for staking – useful in windy locations.

Gardener's tip

Drought-tolerant *Stachys* and *Salvia* are particularly useful in a hot, dry garden. Unlike succulent-like plants such as *Hylotelephium* that retain water, their hairy leaves transpire and the release of moisture has a cooling effect on their immediate environment.

There are plenty of relaxing spots to enjoy a rest with a reviving cuppa

Enjoy your visit

Plan
your day
at rhs.org.uk/wisley

Eating

Whether it's time for a quick coffee, a hearty lunch or a relaxing afternoon tea, there's a welcoming venue to suit. Our talented culinary team prepares homemade dishes in-house daily using seasonal, locally sourced ingredients and, wherever possible, fresh fruit, vegetables and herbs grown on-site. Wherever you are in the garden, you're never far from a delicious moment:

Wisley Café is ideally placed near the garden entrance for a light lunch or coffee break before you explore.

The **Food Hall** serves generous hot and cold meals, signature cakes and drinks including barista-made coffee.

Glasshouse Kitchen is a family-friendly spot offering pizza, pasta and fresh salads.

World Food Café invites you to dine among edible flowers and herbs in the World Food Garden, with a delicious menu inspired by global cuisines.

Stone Pine Café offers lunches in a peaceful retreat at RHS Wisley's northenmost tip, with wonderful views (seasonal opening).

The **Terrace Restaurant** provides a full table-service experience, showcasing the best of local and garden produce for lunch or afternoon tea, overlooking the East Lawn.

Dine among edible flowers in the World Food Café

Stylish dining in the Terrace Restaurant

Shopping

The award-winning RHS Garden Centre Wisley is a must-visit for gardeners and gift-seekers alike, with an exceptional range of plants including houseplants, perennials, alpines, trees, shrubs and roses. Quality tools and accessories as well as seeds, bulbs, planters and pots have been chosen to support sustainable gardening. Should you need help or advice, our fabulously friendly team of staff are on hand, whether you're a beginner, plant collector, or just browsing.

In the shop, you will find beautiful gifts, homewares, fashion and fragrances, many from UK suppliers who share the RHS's sustainability values. Find a comprehensive range of gardening books, along with cookbooks, fiction and children's books.

Don't miss!

'Love it today, Grow it tomorrow' ranges are featured throughout the year, enabling you to replicate many planting combinations seen in RHS Wisley at home.

Showstopping illuminations for RHS Glow at Wisley

Events

RHS Wisley is a vibrant hub of activity with a rolling programme of hundreds of events in all seasons to inspire, educate and entertain. From hands-on workshops to dazzling displays, there's always something new to discover:

Guided garden tours invite you to join expert-led walks through our glorious ever-changing landscape.

Horticultural events provide opportunities to meet expert growers, enjoy live demonstrations and shop from top plant nurseries.

Family trails and activities help children connect with nature through fun, educational adventures.

Workshops and courses offer chances to learn new skills, from beginner gardening to advanced horticulture.

Foodie festivals such as Plot to Plate celebrate the best seasonal produce.

RHS Glow at Wisley transforms the garden into a magical wonderland in a spectacular winter light show.

RHS Garden Wisley Flower Show celebrates horticultural excellence in a six-day extravaganza every September with floral displays, expert talks and plant shopping from top nurseries and tradestands.

See the latest line-up of events at rhs.org.uk/wisleywhatson

There's plenty of family fun to be had

A newly-married couple pose for photos against the tropical backdrop of The Glasshouse

Private hire

RHS Wisley offers a choice of spectacular settings for weddings, stylish corporate gatherings, milestone occasions and filming projects, blending elegance with the beauty of nature. The Glasshouse, an architectural marvel, is an immersive environment with dramatic tropical planting, while RHS Hilltop provides a vast contemporary space with sweeping views. Many other venues are available, all framed by seasonal colour and beautifully curated landscapes to create an unforgettable backdrop for your event. To explore the possibilities and bring your ideas into bloom, contact the team at RHSVenuesWisley@rhs.org.uk

The Garden Room at Hilltop dressed for a wedding reception

Published in 2025 by
Royal Horticultural Society
80 Vincent Square
London SW1P 2PE
020 3176 5800
rhs.org.uk

ISBN 978 191 166 64 62

Reg Charity No. 222879/
SC038262

Editor Emma Kendell

Deputy Art Editor Carly Hurd

Workflow Manager Ally Page

Sub Editor Marina Jordan-Rugg

Head of Editorial Tom Howard

Art Editor Mark Timothy

Photography:
Lee Beel, Richard Bloom, Lee Charlton, Murray Clarke, Tarah Coonan, Paul Debois, Oliver Dixon, Adam Duckworth, Wilf Halliday, Samuel Hall, Neil Hepworth, Jason Ingram, Paul Kettell, Joanna Kossack, Grace Marr, Clive Nichols, James Robert Pullman, Smiemans Projecten, Nicola Stocken, Eli Sutton, Alex Swyer, Mark Waugh, Mark Winwood, Helen Yates

Showstopping illuminations for RHS Glow at Wisley

Events

RHS Wisley is a vibrant hub of activity with a rolling programme of hundreds of events in all seasons to inspire, educate and entertain. From hands-on workshops to dazzling displays, there's always something new to discover:

Guided garden tours invite you to join expert-led walks through our glorious ever-changing landscape.

Horticultural events provide opportunities to meet expert growers, enjoy live demonstrations and shop from top plant nurseries.

Family trails and activities help children connect with nature through fun, educational adventures.

Workshops and courses offer chances to learn new skills, from beginner gardening to advanced horticulture.

Foodie festivals such as Plot to Plate celebrate the best seasonal produce.

RHS Glow at Wisley transforms the garden into a magical wonderland in a spectacular winter light show.

RHS Garden Wisley Flower Show celebrates horticultural excellence in a six-day extravaganza every September with floral displays, expert talks and plant shopping from top nurseries and tradestands.

See the latest line-up of events at rhs.org.uk/wisleywhatson

There's plenty of family fun to be had

Private hire

RHS Wisley offers a choice of spectacular settings for weddings, stylish corporate gatherings, milestone occasions and filming projects, blending elegance with the beauty of nature. The Glasshouse, an architectural marvel, is an immersive environment with dramatic tropical planting, while RHS Hilltop provides a vast contemporary space with sweeping views. Many other venues are available, all framed by seasonal colour and beautifully curated landscapes to create an unforgettable backdrop for your event. To explore the possibilities and bring your ideas into bloom, contact the team at RHSVenuesWisley@rhs.org.uk

The Garden Room at Hilltop dressed for a wedding reception

A newly-married couple pose for photos against the tropical backdrop of The Glasshouse

Published in 2025 by Royal Horticultural Society
80 Vincent Square
London SW1P 2PE
020 3176 5800
rhs.org.uk

ISBN 978 191 166 64 62

Editor Emma Kendell

Deputy Art Editor Carly Hurd

Workflow Manager Ally Page

Sub Editor Marina Jordan-Rugg

Head of Editorial Tom Howard

Art Editor Mark Timothy

Photography:
Lee Beel, Richard Bloom, Lee Charlton, Murray Clarke, Tarah Coonan, Paul Debois, Oliver Dixon, Adam Duckworth, Wilf Halliday, Samuel Hall, Neil Hepworth, Jason Ingram, Paul Kettell, Joanna Kossack, Grace Marr, Clive Nichols, James Robert Pullman, Smiemans Projecten, Nicola Stocken, Eli Sutton, Alex Swyer, Mark Waugh, Mark Winwood, Helen Yates